The Classical Piano Method
Method Book 3

Hans-Günter Heumann

ED 13563

SCHOTT

www.schott-music.com

Mainz · London · Madrid · New York · Paris · Prague · Tokyo · Toronto
© 2014 SCHOTT MUSIC GmbH & Co. KG, Mainz · Printed in Germany

About the author:

Hans-Günter Heumann is a freelance composer and author, living in southern Germany.

Since studying piano, composition, and music pedagogy at the Musikhochschule Hannover, followed by further studies in the USA, he has dedicated himself to the editing of pedagogical piano material. He has a particular interest in presenting music in an accessible way to reach a broad audience.

Based on many years of experience teaching children, young people and adults, Hans-Günter Heumann has written a great number of internationally successful and award winning publications, and has composed and arranged piano music in a range of styles for beginners to advanced students.

Having developed successful, methodical concepts for learning how to play the piano for all age groups and abilities, Hans-Günter Heumann's work has been translated into many different languages and sold millions of copies, an indication of the wide-spread appreciation of his work.
His publications *Klavierspielen – mein schönstes Hobby* and *Piano Kids* (both published by Schott Music) have become two of the most significant piano methods in the German language.

Acknowledgments

The author and publishers would like to thank Carol Klose and our colleagues at Hal Leonard Corporation for expert suggestions, support and advice in the development of *The Classical Piano Method*.

ED 13563
British Library Cataloguing-in-Publication-Data.
A catalogue record for this book is available from the British Library.
ISMN 979-0-2201-3447-0
ISBN 978-1-84761-294-6

Cover design by www.adamhaystudio.com
Cover photography: iStockphoto
Layout and Engraving: www.bbruemmer.de
English translation: Wendy Lampa
Printed in Germany S&Co.8939

Contents

LESSON 11

LESSON 12

Summary of Book 2

Intervals

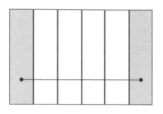

Sixth

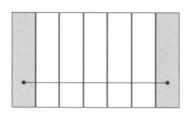

Seventh

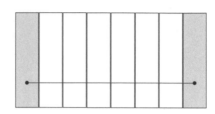

Octave

Dynamics (volume)

sforzato...........**sf**......................a very strong accent

marcato.....................................marked, emphasized

diminuendo......**dim. or dimin.**......Decreasing in volume, becoming softer – same meaning as decrescendo

Tempo (speed)

vivace.............lively, fast

con moto.........with movement, quickly

tranquillo.........tranquil

grazioso...........graceful, charming

espressivo........with expression

a tempo...........return to the previous tempo

adagio.............slowly, unhurried

Time signatures, notes, rests

6/8 time

count: 1   2   3   4   5   6

Sixteenth note =
 Semiquaver

Dotted Eighth note =
 Dotted Quaver

Sixteenth rest =
 Semiquaver Rest

Dotted Eighth rest =
 Dotted Quaver rest

C = 4/4

Octave Transposition Sign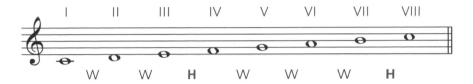

Dal Segno al Fine = _D.S. al Fine_
Dal Segno is an instruction to repeat a piece of music from the sign (𝄋) until the word _Fine_ (= end).

C Major Scale

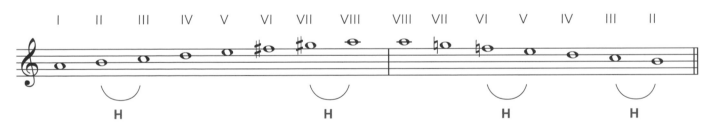

Natural A Minor Scale

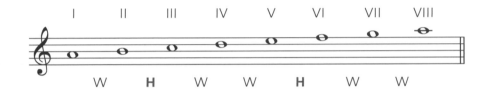

Harmonic A Minor Scale

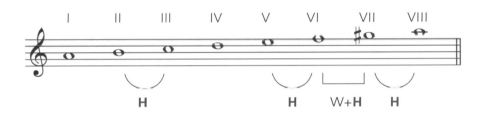

Melodic A Minor Scale

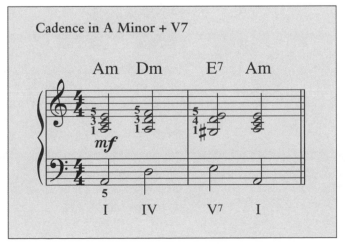

Lesson 1

Song Accompaniment 1

Songs may be accompanied with chords. In Volume 2 of *The Classical Piano Method*, the three primary chords of a key (Step I = Tonic **T**, Step IV = Subdominant **S**, Step V = Dominant **D**) and the Dominant Seventh chord (**V7**) were introduced and practised in cadences (chord sequences).

Here we present a classical melody, with chord symbols added. This simplified form of notation is commonly used in jazz, pop and rock music and is known as a **lead sheet**. Using different patterns for the left hand, you can create interesting accompaniments to the melody.

THE LINDEN TREE / LEAD SHEET

Franz Schubert (1797-1828)

Franz Schubert
(1797-1828)

Country: Austria
Period: Romantic

Schubert's great musical talent was evident from a very early age, and he received his first music lessons from his father. In 1808 he entered the Theological Boarding School of St Stephan's Cathedral in Vienna, as a choir boy, where he was taught by Antonio Salieri amongst others. From 1814-18 he was an assistant teacher at his father's school. From 1818 Schubert lived as a freelance musician, finding, by 1821, musical support and recognition in a circle of friends including musicians, artists and writers, who called their gatherings 'Schubertiads'. Many of his works received their first performances at these events. Schubert never held an official post and gave only one public performance in his lifetime, which was a great success. Amongst his most famous works are the song cycles: *Die schöne Müllerin* (The Beautiful Maid of the Mill), *Winterreise* (Winter Journey), *Schwanengesang* (Song of Swans), the songs *Ave Maria*, *Ständchen*, *Heidenröslein*, the *Unfinished Symphony*, the Piano Quintet *The Trout*, the String Quartet *Death and the Maiden*, piano works such as *Wanderer Fantasy*, Impromptus and Moment musicaux and the *German Mass*.

THE LINDEN TREE / PATTERN 1

The first accompaniment pattern consists of single notes, i.e. the primary notes of the tonic, subdominant and dominant. These low held, or accompanying notes are known as a **bordun** (Fr. bourdon, Ital. bordone = drone). The bordun is an ancient, simple kind of polyphony.

Franz Schubert (1797-1828)
Arr.: Hans-Günter Heumann

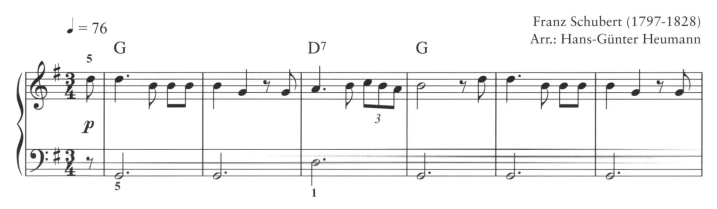

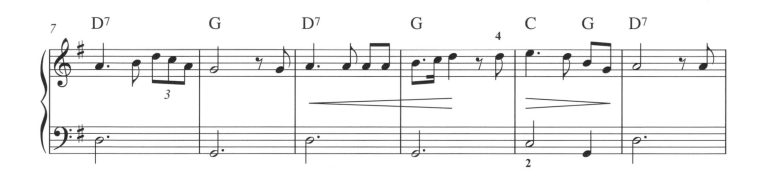

THE LINDEN TREE / PATTERN 2

A bordun can also be played with several notes as, for example, on the bordun string of a hurdy-gurdy or the bordun pipes of the bagpipes, but usually consists of two notes a fifth apart. The bordun fifth can also be played rhythmically.

Franz Schubert (1797-1828)
Arr.: Hans-Günter Heumann

In the following three accompaniment patterns the melody is accompanied by the tonic, subdominant and dominant chords in their inversions.

The notes of the chords are played all together or one after another. Look out for a few exceptions.

THE LINDEN TREE / PATTERN 3

root position   2nd inversion   1st inversion
                                                                            without fifth

THE LINDEN TREE / PATTERN 4

Exceptions:
measure 11   measure 15   measure 17   measure 18

THE LINDEN TREE / PATTERN 5

Exceptions:
measure 10+14   measure 11   measure 17   measure 18

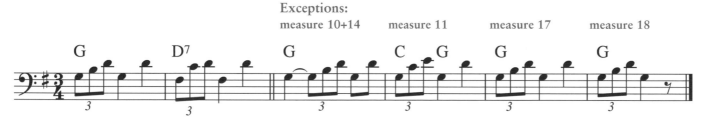

Playing Tips:

Play the melody, and try out the chords, bar by bar, to see which chord fits. There may be a change of chord within a bar.

The upbeat is not harmonized.

A piece usually begins and ends on the tonic.

Compare the notes of the melody with the notes of the primary triads bar by bar, or half a bar at a time. Use the chord which contains one or more of the melody notes. You should hear when the chord sounds correct.

You can recognize the key of a piece by the key signature, and often also by the final note, which is usually the key note or the third of the scale – or simply by the tonal character of the melody.

Lesson 2

D Major Scale

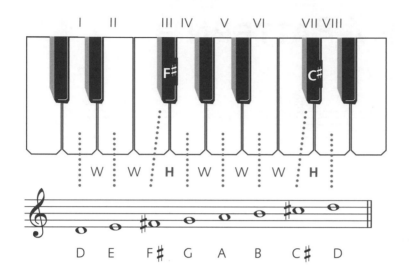

I II III IV V VI VII VIII

W   W   H   W   W   W   H

D   E   F♯   G   A   B   C♯   D

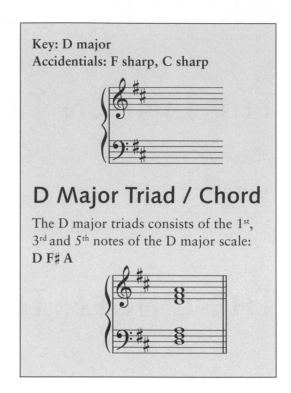

Key: D major
Accidentals: F sharp, C sharp

D Major Triad / Chord

The D major triads consists of the 1st, 3rd and 5th notes of the D major scale: **D F♯ A**

D Major Triad with Inversions

R. H. 5(4) 3(2) 1

L. H. 1 3(2) 5(4)

1 3 5 1 2 5 1 3 5   8⸺   3   5

5 3 1 5 3 1 5 2 1   2   1

Playing Tip:

Play these two exercises with each hand separately then with both hands together. Begin with the L.H. one octave lower, or two octaves lower for the broken chords.

Perfect Cadence in D Major with Inversions

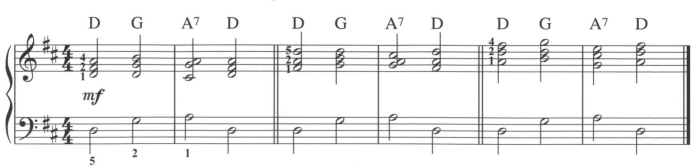

D   G   A⁷   D   D   G   A⁷   D   D   G   A⁷   D

mf

FINGER FITNESS 1

Hans-Günter Heumann

COUNTRY DANCE

Ländler, WoO 11, No. 4

Ludwig van Beethoven (1770-1827)

Ländler is the term for an Austro-Bavarian folk dance from around 1800 in a gentle 3/4-time. It consists of two repeated 8-bar sections. Mozart, Beethoven and Schubert adopted the Ländler into their compositions.

Beethoven published these dances without opus numbers (WoO = work without opus number) for orchestra as well as for piano solo.

RC+DC+FF More pieces in **Repertoire Collection**, **Duet Collection** and **Finger Fitness**, see page 107

Musette

from the *Notebook for Anna Magdalena Bach*

Anonymous
BWV Anh.126

Fine

D.C. al Fine

Lesson 3

Song Accompaniment 2
Lullaby / Lead Sheet Op. 49, No. 4

Johannes Brahms (1833-1897)

Patterns for the Left Hand

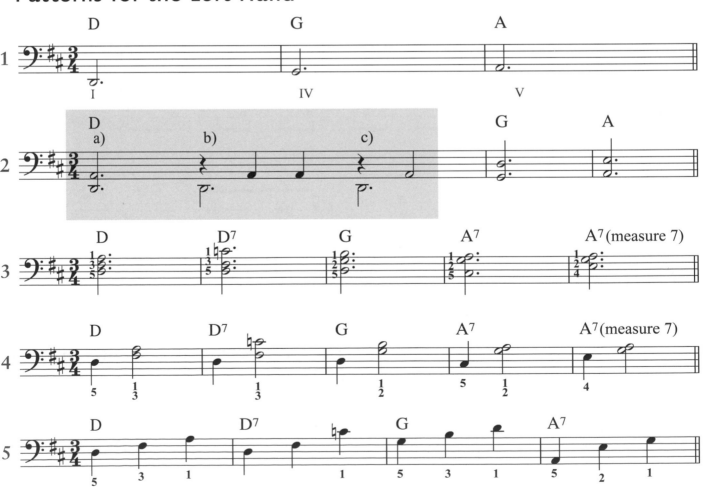

LULLABY / PATTERN 5

Johannes Brahms (1833-1897)
Arr.: Hans-Günter Heumann

■ Playing Tip:

You are now able to accompany many well-known melodies in this way. For example, play the melody of the folk song *Red River Valley*, by ear, in C major, and accompany it with the pattern you have learnt.

Begin with the note G. Try the same thing with *Happy Birthday*, but this time in the key of G major, beginning on D. Both pieces begin with an upbeat that is not harmonized.

Johannes Brahms
(1833-1897)

Country: Germany
Period: Romantic

Brahms was first taught by his father, a double bass player in the city orchestra. He soon began playing the piano in public houses at the harbour to earn money for his family. He later accompanied one of the most famous Hungarian violinists. Brahms was close friends with Robert Schumann, who made him famous with a glowing review, and his wife Clara – a celebrated pianist. In 1862 he moved to Vienna where he held several posts (choir conductor, court pianist, concert master), and continued to work as a freelance artist. He presented his compositions in many concerts at home and abroad. Brahms composed 4 symphonies, 2 piano concertos, 1 violin concerto, choral works, chamber music, piano pieces and songs. Amongst his most well-known works are: Piano Concerto No. 1, *A German Requiem*, *Hungarian Dances* for Piano / Orchestra, Waltzes for Piano Duet Op. 39 and Lullaby.

FF ➤ More pieces in **Finger Fitness**, see page 107

Lesson 4

B Minor Scales

Natural B Minor Scale

D Major Scale

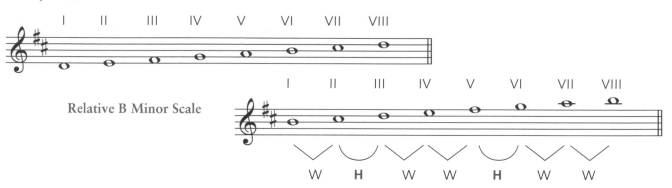

Relative B Minor Scale

B Minor Triad/Chord

The B minor triad consists of the 1st, 3rd and 5th notes of the B minor scale: B D F♯

Key: B minor
Key signature: F sharp, C sharp (as in D major)

Harmonic B Minor Scale

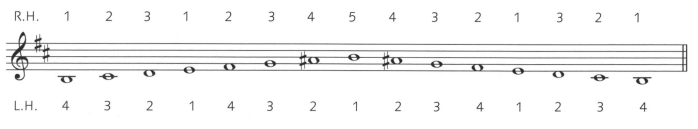

Melodic B Minor Scale

FINGER FITNESS 2

Hans-Günter Heumann

AFTER THE BALL

Op 98, No. 13

Alexander Gretchaninov (1864-1956)

The **Mazurka** is a traditional polish dance in a lively 3/4-time. Subdivision of the first beat (e.g. dotted quarter note) is a typical feature, as is the displacement of emphasis to the second beat. Frédéric Chopin (1810-1849) introduced the Mazurka into classical music.

■ Playing Tip:

The tempo of a piece does not always remain exactly the same throughout but may be varied to a certain extent, depending on the performer's taste and feeling for style.

In the piece *After the Ball* by Gretchaninov, a few tempo indications are given, which contribute to the expressive nature of the piece.

Examples of variations in tempo:

rallentando, rall. or **rallent.** = getting slower
ritardando, rit. or **ritard.** = getting slower
ritenuto, riten. = hold back, hesitate
stringendo, string. = gradually getting faster (squeezing, tightening)
accelerando, accel. = gradually getting faster (speed up)

Agogics

Agogics is the generic term for changes of tempo that bring a composition to life. Although the performer should in principle keep to the performance directions as indicated, the directions leave a certain amount of artistic freedom. For example, there may be slight variations in tempo at melodic or harmonic climaxes, where leaps occur, at the end of a musical section or during a slur, where the first note may be stretched a little.

Tempo rubato also falls in this category (Ital. rubare = to steal), whereby notes with the same rhythmic value may be played unequally, or with a slightly slower or faster tempo. However, variation of the tempo is to be dealt with very carefully and only in certain compositions.

Alexander Gretchaninov (1864-1956)

Country: Russia
Period: 20th Century

Gretchaninov studied at the Conservatoires in Moscow and St Petersburg. From 1925 he lived in Paris; from 1939 in the USA. In 1946 he received US citizenship. As he was closely connected with tradition, his works sound rather conservative. He composed orchestral works, concertos, operas, vocal music, chamber music and piano music. Gretchaninov wrote works especially for children such as piano pieces, and operas. He had a particular gift for creating simple, melodic, expressive music that captured the imagination of children, for example in Op. 98, Op. 99 and Op. 119.

RC+DC+FF ▶ More pieces in **Repertoire Collection, Duet Collection** and **Finger Fitness**, see page 107

Lesson 5

B♭ Major Scale

▢ Playing Tips:

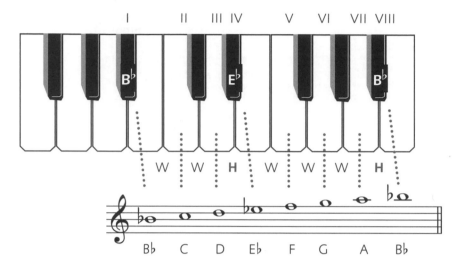

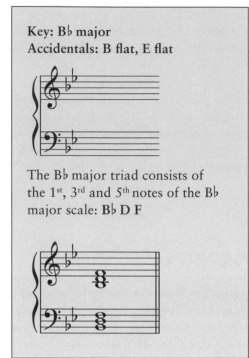

Key: B♭ major
Accidentals: B flat, E flat

The B♭ major triad consists of the 1st, 3rd and 5th notes of the B♭ major scale: B♭ D F

B♭ Major Triad with Inversions

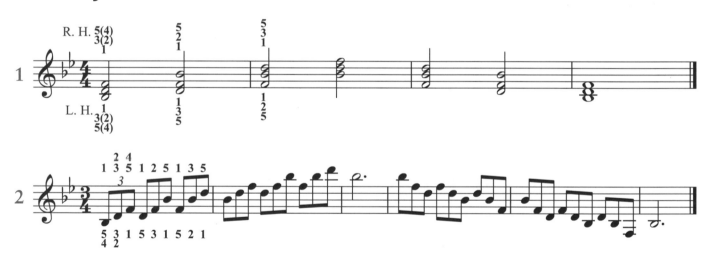

▢ Playing Tip:

Play these two exercises with each hand separately then with both hands together. Begin with the L.H. one octave lower, or two octaves lower for the broken chords.

Perfect Cadence in B♭ Major with Inversions

FINGER FITNESS 3

from *Instructive Practice Pieces for Pianoforte*

August Eberhard Müller (1767-1817)

August Eberhard Müller (1767-1817)

Country: Germany
Period: Classical

Müller was a teacher, organist, pianist and composer, who was highly regarded during his lifetime. From 1804 he was cantor at St Thomas Church in Leipzig – a position that was previously held by Johann Sebastian Bach, amongst others, and *Kapellmeister* in Weimar. Müller composed for flute as well as piano. For piano he wrote, for example, two concertos, 10 sonatas and a successful fortepiano method.

Allegro

K3

Wolfgang Amadeus Mozart (1756-1791)

The Appoggiatura

The **appoggiatura** is a small note that is written before the main note. It begins on the beat of the main note, and shortens this accordingly.

The duration of the appoggiatura is generally half the value of the main note, or two-thirds if it is a dotted note.

Portato (Ital. portare = to carry)

Portato is a performance direction meaning sustained, but not legato. It is a form of articulation whereby the notes should be played neither staccato (short, separated) nor legato (joined smoothly), but each note should be played with a little emphasis. A sequence of notes should be noticeably separated from one another, but not as short as staccato. Portato is therefore similar to the indication *non legato*.

usually written   or   or

Mozart's compositions do not usually give performance directions, so it is left to the interpreter to choose the appropriate articulation, dynamics and fingering. This Allegro K3, composed on March 4th 1762, at the age of 6, was probably written under the supervision of his father Leopold. The performance directions given in this piece should be used as a guide to interpretation. To achieve a differentiation in sound it is advisable to practise with each hand separately, very slowly. Furthermore, the longer notes (crotchets/quarter notes) should be clearly detached from one another (portato), as notated in the first bar, for example. Play using the weight of the arm, and with a slower wrist movement than in staccato playing.

Due to the dynamic range of the early pianoforte, the **terrace dynamics** range from forte to piano. A sudden dynamic change is effective here and is stylistically appropriate for music of that era.

Changing finger on the same note as seen from bar 13 onwards is an ideal way of supporting the indicated articulation. The appoggiatura (bars 9 and 27) begins on the beat of the main note (and is therefore played with emphasis) and reduces the duration of that note to half its value.

RC+DC+FF ▶ More pieces in **Repertoire Collection**, **Duet Collection** and **Finger Fitness**, see page 107

Lesson 6

G Minor Scales

Natural G Minor Scale

B♭ Major Scale

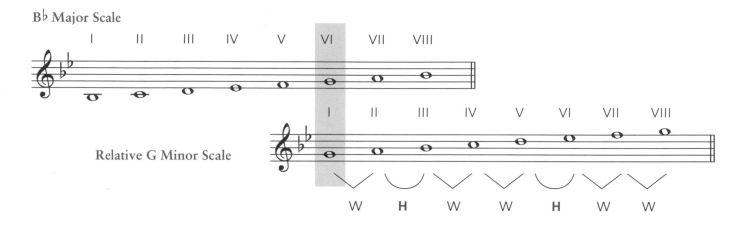

G Minor Triad/Chord

The G minor triad consists of the 1ˢᵗ, 3ʳᵈ and 5ᵗʰ notes of the G minor scale: G B♭ D

Key: G minor
Key signature: B flat, E flat (same as B♭ major)

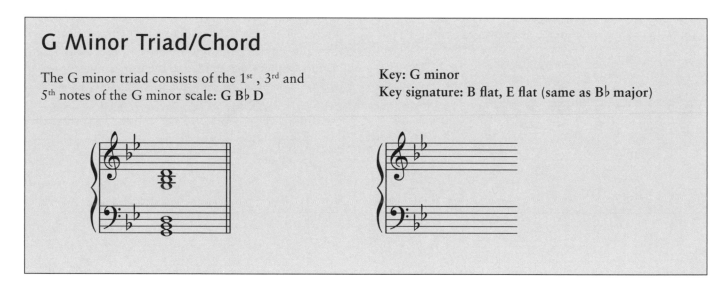

Harmonic G Minor Scale

Melodic G Minor Scale

FINGER FITNESS 4

Hans-Günter Heumann

Extending the range

It is usual for up to 4 or 5 ledger lines to be used in piano music.

THE SICK DOLL

from *Children's Album* Op. 39, No. 6

Pyotr Ilyich Tchaikovsky (1840-1893)

Exercises for Finger Independence

■ Technique Tip:

These so-called *tie exercises* help to achieve independence of the fingers. One finger presses a key down and keeps it held down – as though it is tied down – while the other fingers play.

Frédéric Chopin liked to use these types of exercises in similar hand positions, as they fitted the hand position in the most natural way. The long fingers play the black keys; the shorter fingers play the white keys.

Note: Play these slowly, with each hand separately first, then with both hands together. Keep the wrist and arm relaxed. Concentrate on exercising each finger separately.

Minuet

K 88d

Domenico Scarlatti (1685-1757)

RC+DC+FF ➤ More pieces in **Repertoire Collection**, **Duet Collection** and **Finger Fitness**, see page 107

Theory Check 1

1. What is a *Bordun*?

2. Add a drone fifth above the following notes:

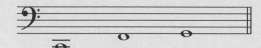

3. Add the appropriate chord symbols:

4. How many public concerts did Franz Schubert give in his lifetime? _____

5. Complete the four-part cadence:

6. What notes make up the B♭ minor triad?

— — —

7. Give two terms each for the following changes in tempo: getting slower, getting faster:

_____ _____ ,

_____ _____

8. How is this appoggiatura played?

9. Which form of articulation is played neither legato nor staccato?

_____

10. Which composer supported the young Johannes Brahms and made him famous almost overnight through positive reviews in his magazine, published by one of the leading music publishers?

_____

See page 98 for answers

Domenico Scarlatti
(1685-1757)

Country: Italy
Period: Baroque

Domenico Scarlatti was born in the same year as Bach und Handel, and was the son of the famous composer Alessandro Scarlatti. In 1709 he became *Kapellmeister* in Rome, in 1720 he taught the young child Maria Barbara at the Portuguese court. After she married, he followed her to Seville and Madrid, working as her harpsichordist. Scarlatti wrote over 550 pieces for harpsichord, which he called Sonatas, Essercizi and Pièces pour le clavecin. In this way he established himself as a specialist piano composer and developed a previously unknown virtuoso technique. These pieces show a preference for two-part writing.
He also wrote operas, oratorios, cantatas and further sacred works.

Lesson 7
Sight-Reading

● Sight-reading is the simultaneous reading, playing, and perhaps also interpreting of a piece of music without having practised it beforehand.

● Sight-reading is an important part of the pianist's training and should be included as a feature of regular practice from the early stages of learning.

● This security in reading from notation, gained over time, will be useful to you in many ways, for example, in accompanying another instrumentalist or singer, as well as in learning to play new piano pieces.

● Sight-reading should begin with one hand, then progress to two. You should always sight-read pieces easier than those that represent the level you have achieved in your studies.

Preparation for Sight-Reading:

1. **Key signature, time signature and accidentals**
   Count along with the beat and count a complete bar before you begin

2. **Hand position**
   How does the piece begin? Place your hands in the correct position.

3. **Look at the music, not at the keys**
   Looking back and forth from the music to the keyboard takes too much time and prevents you from looking ahead at the music.

4. **Find the keys silently**
   Finding the groups of two and three black notes, silently, with your eyes closed or without looking at the keyboard (see Volume 1, p. 16/18) helps you to locate the white keys.

5. **Direction, distance between notes, duration**
   Quickly think through the ascending and descending movement of the notes, the intervals (repeated notes, stepwise movements, leaps) as well as the durations, and concentrate more on the problematic parts. Keep a look out for patterns and repetition.

   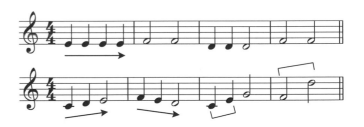

6. **Tempo**
   Play sight-reading pieces slowly and try to keep going without hesitation, even if it means missing notes, or playing wrong ones.

FF ▷ More pieces in **Finger Fitness**, see page 108

Playing Tip:

For the following five examples, choose a slow tempo so that you can play through without hesitating. Before you begin playing, take note of all the preparation points on the opposite page. It is very important to look ahead at the music whilst playing.

Hans-Günter Heumann

Lesson 8
Classical Crash Course 1

Stylistic Period: Baroque

In music and art the **period from c. 1600-1750 is known as the Baroque era** (Portuguese *barroco* = irregular, askew). The term was coined around 1800 and indicates, perhaps deprecatingly, the complicated and ornamented musical language of this time, which the new generation found turgid and flamboyant. From the late 19th century, however, the Baroque period was regarded very positively.

Basso continuo (continuous, unbroken bass) is the term for a continuous bass accompaniment to a melody. The harpsichordist or organist plays the bass line and adds chords according to particular rules. To help, there are figures given beneath the bass part. The basso continuo is a type of short hand or numerical script, similar to the chord symbols commonly used today. The figures give the intervals of the notes that should be played above the bass note. This means of notation is also known as **figured bass**.

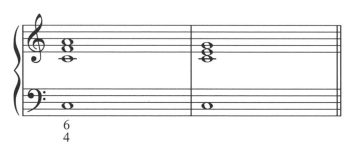

6
4

In figured bass the numbering $\begin{smallmatrix}6\\4\end{smallmatrix}$ indicates that the performer should play a chord with a bass note (notated) + the 4th and 6th above this.

No numbers indicate a triad with a bass note (notated) + the 3rd and 5th above this.

> ## Features of the Baroque Period
>
> - Basso Continuo
> - The Concerto grosso
> - Ornamentation
> - Polyphony

The use of figured bass was so typical for the Baroque era that it is also referred to as the **figured bass period**.

The **Concerto grosso** is the main form used in baroque instrumental music. The main orchestra (*Tutti,* Ital. = all) and a small instrumental group, the so-called *Concertino,* play alternately. The Concertino usually consists of three solo instruments, e.g. two violins (or flutes, oboes) and cello (or harpsichord).

Ornamentation is the embellishment and rhythmic alteration of melodies, usually indicated by particular symbols or smaller notes. In the Baroque period there was a real boom in the practice of ornamentation. The melodic framework was brought to life, and single notes were ornamented to enrich the sound and artistry of the music.

Polyphony (Greek *polyphonia* = many voices) is the term for pieces in many parts in which the individual parts, or voices, are melodically and rhythmically independent. The most important polyphonic forms are the *canon* and the *fugue.*

Important Musical Forms of Baroque Music

◯ **Opera**
The opera was created around 1600 in Florence, where a group of well-educated men – the *Florentine Camerata* – met, to bring Greek drama to life once more. The first opera of significance, *L'Orfeo,* was written by Claudio Monteverdi in 1607 in Italy and the first opera house was opened in Venice in 1637.

◯ **Oratorio**
The oratorio is a composition in several movements for choir, single voices (soloists) and orchestra, similar in form to the opera, but usually with religious themes. A narrator tells the story in recitative (speech song). Orchestral interludes, arias and choral sections complete the oratorio, which is performed as a concert. The most well-known oratorio is the *Messiah* by G. F. Handel.

◯ **Cantata**
The cantata is a vocal work in several move ments with instrumental accompaniment. The texts may be sacred or secular. It is similar to the oratorio, but on a smaller scale. J. S. Bach wrote over 200 works of this kind.

◯ **Concerto grosso** (see p. 34)

◯ **Suite**
The suite is a composition in many parts, consisting of a series of dances, for example: *Allemande, Courante, Sarabande, Gigue* and *Minuet*. One of the most famous works of this kind is the *Water Music* by G. F. Handel.

◯ **Fugue**
The fugue is a piece of music with several voices (a polyphonic work) which adheres to strict rules and requires great skill to compose. It begins in one voice, with the introduction of the theme. Once completed, the second voice restates the theme at an interval of a fifth, while the opening voice, according to the rules, develops a 'counter' voice, or 'counterpoint'. The same thing happens at the entry of each further voice. A fugue does not usually have more than four voices. **Fughetta** is the term for a little fugue.
J.S. Bach was a master of the fugue.

Keyboard instruments of the Baroque Period

Clavichord, harpsichord, spinet, virginal, organ

Famous Baroque Composers

Claudio Monteverdi (1567-1643)

Heinrich Schütz (1585-1672)

Jean-Baptiste Lully (1632-1687)

Arcangelo Corelli (1653-1713)

Henry Purcell (1659-1695)

Antonio Vivaldi (c. 1678-1749)

Georg Philipp Telemann (1681-1767)

Jean-Philippe Rameau (1683-1764)

Johann Sebastian Bach (1685-1750)

Domenico Scarlatti (1685-1757)

George Frideric Handel (1685-1759)

Opera

OMBRA MAI FÙ

from the opera *Serse* HWV 40

George Frideric Handel (1685-1759)
Arr.: Hans-Günter Heumann

Pedal in Baroque Music

Harpsichords are rich in overtones and do not have pedals. The effect of a pedal is achieved by the use of finger legato. The harmony notes are also often held longer than notated. On the modern piano the pedal is hardly used in the interpretation of baroque music, unless it is specifically to produce overtones and a fuller sound.

Playing Tip:

It is possible to play legato with the outer fingers even without the use of the thumb. Crossing the 4th finger over the 5th, for example (see bars 4 and 19) and crossing the 5th finger under the 4th (see bar 12) was typical in the early baroque period, when runs on the keyboard were still played without the use of the thumb. Johann Sebastian Bach was the first to use the thumb in runs, but otherwise the use of the thumb was generally restricted to large stretches and chords. The reason for this was that the keys of the instruments at that time were very short, and so the fingers were uncomfortably bent when the thumb was used. This changed with the introduction of the hammer-action piano, where the thumb gained equal importance.

Oratorio

PREPARE THYSELF, ZION

Aria from the *Christmas Oratorio* BWV 248

Johann Sebastian Bach (1685-1750)
Arr.: Hans-Günter Heumann

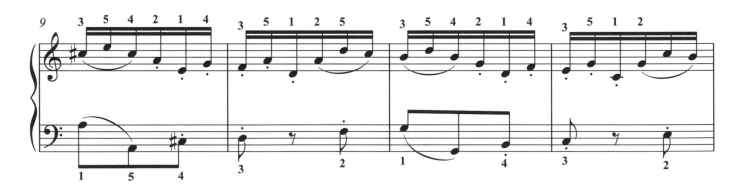

⬜ Playing Tip:

Finger Fitness 5 is a preliminary exercise for the piece by Bach on the opposite page. As bars 9-12 are challenging both technically and in terms of articulation, these should be practised intensively and with different variations. This exercise is relevant as we are dealing with a so-called **sequence** – a musical figure that is repeated, stepwise, at a higher or lower level of pitch. This means that bars 9 and 10 are identical in shape to bars 11 and 12. In the process of working on these exercises, you should learn to play these 4 bars from memory.

FINGER FITNESS 5

Hans-Günter Heumann

FINGER FITNESS 6

Trill Exercise

Hans-Günter Heumann

Thirty-second Note / Demisemiquaver

○ The thirty-second note has a filled note head with a stem and three flags:

○ Two or more thirty-second notes are joined by three beams:

Playing Tips: Trill exercise

Work only at the speed whereby you can be in absolute control, no faster! Choose a very slow tempo to begin with so that you can maintain the tempo as the note values change. Gradually increase the tempo and work through the whole exercise with a metronome.

Listen carefully while you play, to ensure that the trills are even dynamically and rhythmically.

These preliminary exercises are very effective for acquiring a better feeling for the beat while playing trills. This will help you to play them correctly, with confidence.

Technique Tip:

Minimal arm weight
Fingers very close to the keyboard

Cantata

ZION HEARS THE WATCHMEN CALLING

from Cantata No. 140 *Awake, the voice commands*

Johann Sebastian Bach (1685-1750)
Arr.: Hans-Günter Heumann

Dynamics in Baroque Music

Dynamic markings were not usual until the middle of the 18th century. If they were added, they were limited to single indications such as *forte* and *piano*. In fact it was not possible to achieve subtle gradations of dynamics on the harpsichord and organ, as was possible on other instruments. It was therefore common practice in the baroque period to achieve a crescendo or diminuendo between passages or notes using so-called **terrace dynamics** (abrupt, stepwise dynamics). The range of dynamics was not as great at that time as it is on modern instruments.

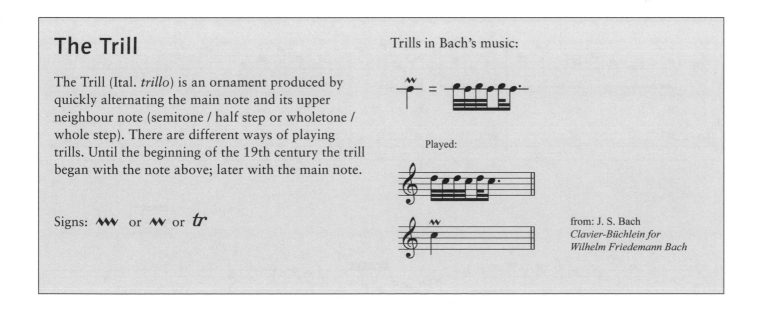

PRELUDE

BWV 939

Johann Sebastian Bach (1685-1750)

Tempo in Baroque Music

Exact tempo markings according to Mälzels metronome (see Volume 1, p. 39) were introduced in 1816. Before this, approximate tempo indications given by the composers – such as allegro, andante, largo – were the only references to how quickly or slowly a piece should be played.

The tempo indications of the time cannot be directly transferred to modern practice, as baroque tempo indications were not precise. The words served to indicate the affect, i.e. the emotional conditions such as happiness, sadness, seriousness or cheerfulness. In the 17th and 18th centuries the means of measuring tempo were inaccurate, for example, a pendulum or even a human pulse might have been used.

Deciding on the Tempo

Affect
The tempo indication often refers to the mood, upon which the tempo is based.

Time signature
The smaller the denominator, the slower the tempo. For example, 3/8-time should be played faster than 3/4-time.

Emphasis within a bar
The more emphases there are in a bar, the slower the tempo.

The smallest note value
The smallest note values in a piece must be able to be played precisely, and audibly.

The Mordent

The Mordent (Fr. *mordant*) is an ornament consisting of a simple change from the main note to the lower neighbour note and back again.

Symbol: ᴧᴧ

A chromatic change is notated with an accidental beneath the mordent (♯).

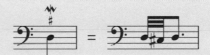

Concerto grosso

PASTORALE

Theme from Concerto grosso Op. 6, No. 8

Arcangelo Corelli (1653-1713)
Arr.: Hans-Günter Heumann

Playing Tip:

In *Pastorale* by Corelli, play the quarter notes (crotchets) portato in the left hand.

The articulation in the right hand often requires slurring two or three notes together. Pay attention to the emphasis on, and also the length of the first note (see p. 49, *Articulation in the Baroque period*).

FINGER FITNESS 7

Hans-Günter Heumann

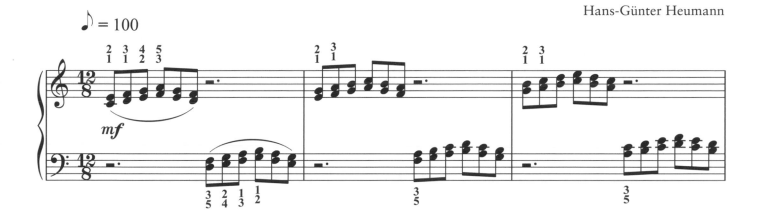

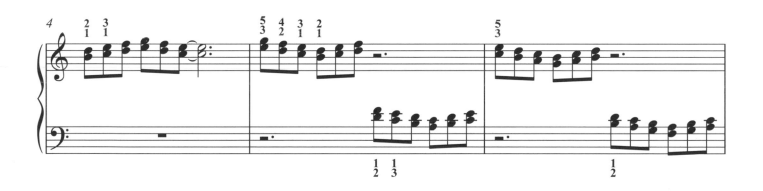

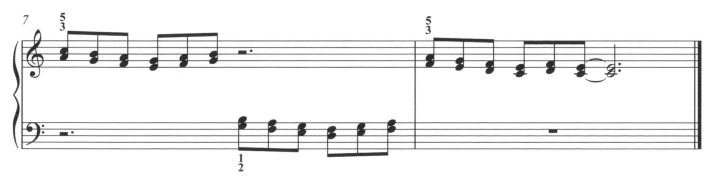

Suite

SARABANDE

from Suite D Minor HWV 448

George Frideric Handel (1685-1759)

Articulation in the Baroque Period

Articulation means the joining and separating of notes. In baroque notation very few markings were given, this was left to the interpreter.

Generally, the following applies: if there is a legato slur, the first note has a certain significance and should be emphasised as well as held a little. It is also worth noting that runs were not performed exactly evenly, but some notes were lengthened slightly, as indicated by slurs, and according to the character played irregularly. You should, however, first play every baroque piece exactly in tempo before trying out these stylistic refinements.

The **Sarabande** is a courtly festive, stately dance in 3/2- or 3/4-time with a characteristic emphasis on the 2nd beat. From 1650-1750 it was a fixed part of the suite.

Fugue

FUGHETTA

from *Seven Fughettas for Harpsichord or Organ*
HWV 611, No. 1

George Frideric Handel (1685-1759)

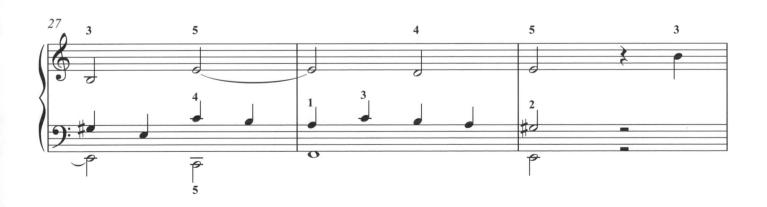

RC+DC+FF ▶ More pieces in **Repertoire Collection, Duet Collection** and **Finger Fitness**, see page 108

Theory Check 2

1. Explain the term polyphony: _____

2. Name four characteristics of the baroque period: _____, _____, _____,
   _____

3. In the concerto grosso the full orchestra (tutti) plays alternately with the: _____.

4. Which of these four composers were famous in the Baroque period: Bach, Mozart, Haydn or Vivaldi?
   _____

5. Give another term for the Baroque period: _____

6. Name a polyphonic piece: _____

7. Who composed the first famous opera in 1607? _____

8. Draw a 32nd note (demisemiquaver): _____

9. What is a sequence? _____

10. Until the beginning of the 19th century, the trill began with the _____ .

11. What is the name of the ornament that consists of a simple alternation of the main note and the lower
    neighbour note? _____

12. Were exact articulation, dynamic and tempo indications given in the original notation of baroque
    compositions? _____

13. What is the general rule regarding tempo in relation to time signature in the baroque period?
    _____

14. What does the term 'affect' mean in baroque music? _____

15. Name the five keyboard instruments of the baroque period: _____, _____, _____, _____,
    _____

16. Who composed the oratorio, *Messiah*? _____

17. What is the name of the compositional form consisting of a series of dances? _____

18. Opera was created around 1600 in Florence. What is the name of the group of well-educated men who
    met to bring Greek drama to life once more? _____

19. An oratorio is a composition in several sections for choir, soloists and orchestra. A narrator tells the
    story, usually based on biblical themes. What is the term for *speech song*? _____

20. In which form did J. S. Bach compose over 200 works? One of the famous examples of this genre is
    No. 147 *My Heart, My Lips, My Deeds, My Life*. _____

See page 98 for answers

Lesson 9
Chromatic Scale

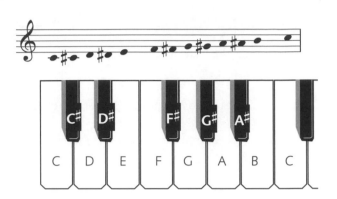

- The **chromatic scale** (Greek *chroma* = colour) consists only of half tones (semitones). It ascends and descends, uses every key, and may begin on any note.

- If there is a series of semitone steps in a melody, this is known as **chromaticism**.

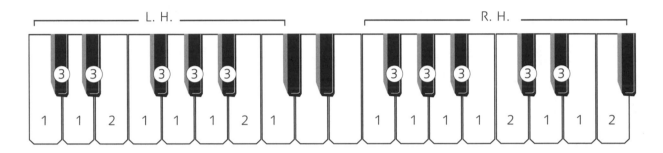

Playing Tip:

3rd finger on the black key; 1st finger on the white key, except where there are two white keys a semitone apart, in which case the fingering is 1-2 or 2-1.

Playing Tip:

Play with each hand separately, then together. Play the chromatic scale beginning on different notes. The left hand plays an octave lower than notated.

FINGER FITNESS 8

Hans-Günter Heumann

ENTRY OF THE GLADIATORS

Theme from Op. 68

Julius Fučík (1872-1916)
Arr.: Hans-Günter Heumann

Tempo di marcia ♩ = 88

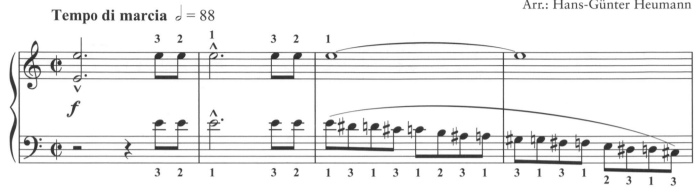

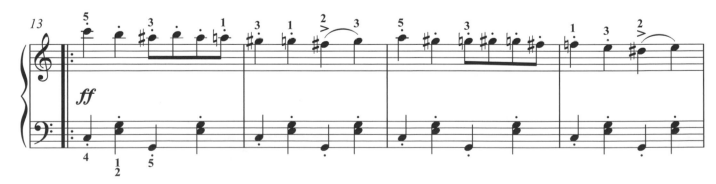

FF ▶ More pieces in **Finger Fitness,** see page 108

Julius Fučík
(1872-1916)

Country:
Czech Republic
Period: Romantic

Fučík studied composition with Antonín Dvořák. In 1891 he began military service. In 1895 he was appointed as second bassoonist at the German Theatre in Prague and in 1896 became conductor of the Prague city theatre. His career as a military musician began in 1897. Over 400 works by Fučík are in existence. His most famous piece, the 'Entry of the Gladiators' (also known as the 'March of the Gladiators'), is known by so many as it is in the repertoire of circus orchestras all over the world.

Lesson 10
Classical Crash Course 2

Stylistic Period: Classical

The term classical means something accomplished, or exemplary in art, literature and music. In music history **the Classical period was from c. 1750-1820.** The term *classical music* nowadays generally refers to European art music in general as opposed to jazz, rock and pop.

The most well-known Classical composers are Joseph Haydn, Wolfgang Amadeus Mozart and Ludwig van Beethoven. As these three musicians lived in Vienna, this is also known as the **Viennese classical period.**

In contrast to the polyphony of the Baroque period, **homophony** (Greek *homos* = the same, unison) is a type of musical texture in which all voices are synchronized, or a melody is accompanied by chords. So, one voice leads, and the others follow.

Famous Classical Composers

Christoph Willibald Gluck (1714-1787)

Joseph Haydn (1732-1809)

Luigi Boccherini (1743-1805)

Antonio Salieri (1750- 1825)

Muzio Clementi (1752- 1832)

Wolfgang Amadeus Mozart (1756-1791)

Ludwig van Beethoven (1770-1827)

Johann Nepomuk Hummel (1778-1837)

Anton Diabelli (1781-1858)

Louis Spohr (1784-1859)

Important Musical Forms of Classical Music

Sonata
The sonata (Ital. *sonare* = to sound) plays a very important role in the Classical period. It consists of three or four movements (movement = a complete section of a composition). The first movement is generally in so-called *sonata form*, which consists of three sections: first two contrasting themes are presented one after another (*exposition*), then developed (*development*) and finally repeated (*recapitulation*). In a four-movement sonata, the third movement is a dance – usually a minuet. There are many sonatas, for example for piano, violin, or other melodic instruments. A short, easy sonata is known as a *sonatina*.

Symphony
The symphony (Greek *symphonia* = sounding together) was developed in the middle of the 18th century, into an orchestral work with three or four movements in different tempos. Joseph Haydn is regarded as the father of the symphony.

Solo concerto
Since the late 18th century, the concerto has been a work in several movements for solo instruments with orchestra. There are, for example, concertos for piano, violin, flute, clarinet and oboe. In the concerto, the full potential of the solo instrument is presented through playing in dialogue with, and alternately as part of the orchestra. The solo cadenza, especially, at the end of the first movement, is an opportunity for the soloist to demonstrate their virtuosity.

String quartet
In a quartet, four musicians play together, each performing an individual part. If two violinists, a viola player and cellists play together this is called a *string quartet*. The Classical form of the string quartet was established primarily by Joseph Haydn.

The Classical Orchestra

The Classical orchestra of Haydn and Mozart around 1790 consisted of the following instruments:

2 Flutes
2 Oboes
2 Clarinets (newly introduced in the classical period)
2 Bassoons
2 Horns
2 Trumpets
2 Timpani
1st and 2nd Violins, Viola, Violoncello, Double Bass (several)

For Beethoven's symphonies the orchestra was extended to include the piccolo, contrabassoon, trombones, triangle, cymbal and bass drum. The smaller chamber orchestra was still used in addition to the symphony orchestra.

The Classical Keyboard Instrument

The era of the grand piano began in the middle of the 18th century

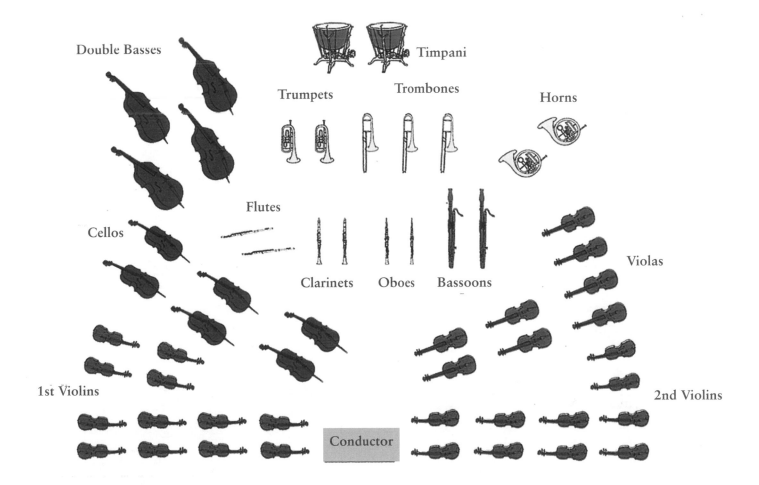

Sonata

SONATINA in C major

Op. 36, No. 1

1st Movement
Exposition

Muzio Clementi (1752-1832)

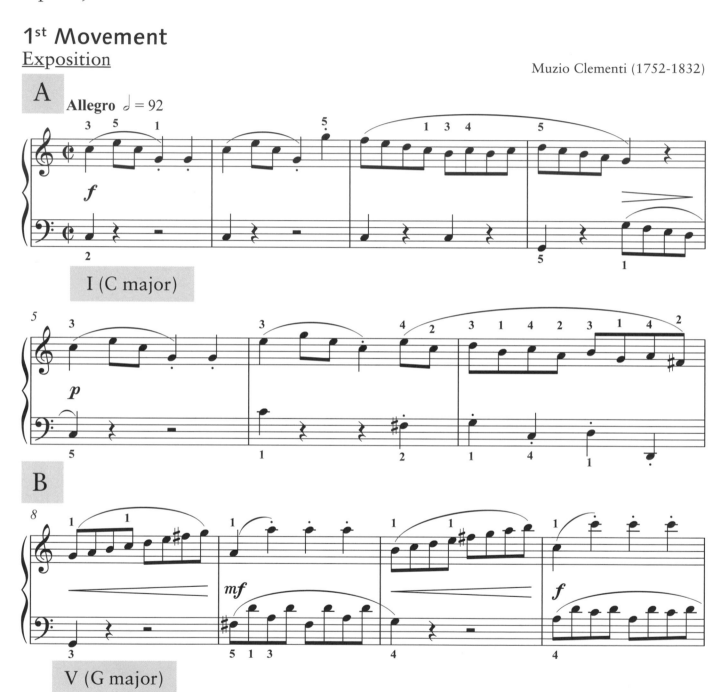

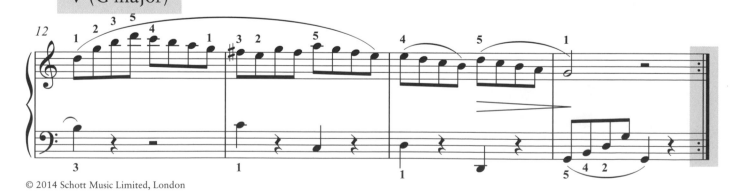

Form and Analysis: Clementi's Sonatina Op. 39, No. 1, 1st Movement

The first movement of this sonatina by Clementi is a perfect example of so-called *sonata form* – as used in the first movement of a sonata. It consits of an:

Exposition, Development and **Recapitulation.**

However, as the name *Sonatina* suggests, everything appears on a smaller scale than in the sonata. Long bridge passages, repeated sections and development in other keys are generally not used.

The **exposition** (bars 1-15) consists of two themes. Theme A (bars 1-7) is in the tonic (C major) and theme B (bars 8-15) in the dominant (G major). The exposition ends with a repeat sign.

In the **development** section (bars 16-23) the themes are explored further. The development usually begins in the dominant, or another key other than the tonic. The key of the development is C minor in this case, and begins with a dominant seventh chord – G7.

The **recapitulation** (bars 24-38) brings back both themes, this time in the tonic, i.e. in C major. The development and recapitulation are repeated.

Playing Tip:

This movement is very cheerful, happy, light hearted and rhythmic with few dissonant harmonies. Pay attention to the dynamics and articulation, in particular the many staccato notes.

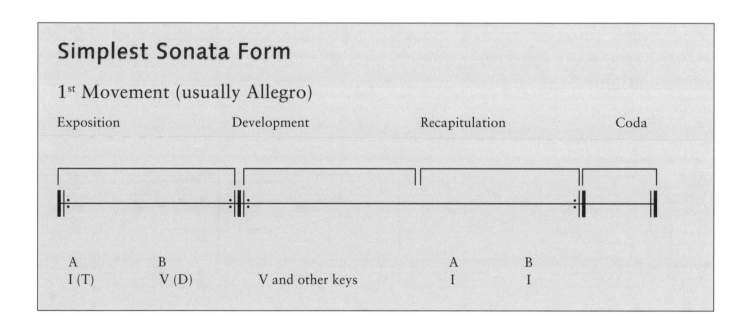

Simplest Sonata Form

1st Movement (usually Allegro)

Exposition	Development	Recapitulation	Coda

| A | B | | A | B | |
| I (T) | V (D) | V and other keys | I | I | |

Development

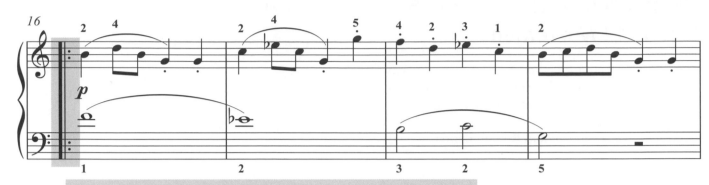

V and other keys (e. g. in this case: C minor)

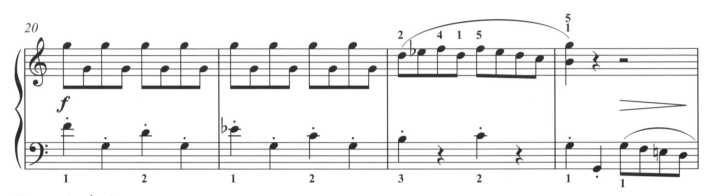

Recapitulation

A

I (C major)

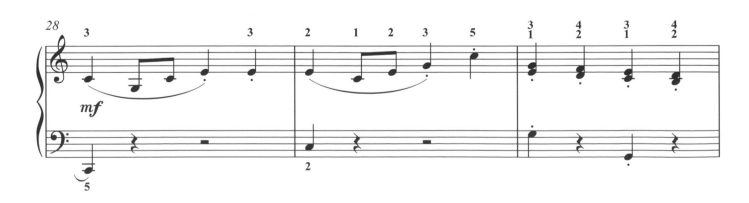

B

I (C major)

Muzio Clementi
(1752-1832)

Country: Italy
Period: Classical

Clementi was a virtuoso harpsichordist and organist by the age of 9 and received his first position in his home city, Rome. At the age of 14 a rich Englishman took him to his estate and enabled the young Clementi to receive a comprehensive education. In 1774 he gave his first public concert in London and achieved great acclaim. From 1780 he made several European tours and, amongst other things, a piano contest with Mozart in Vienna ended in a draw, in the presence of the Kaiser. His completely new, powerful way of playing caused a stir wherever he performed. His grave in Westminster Abbey in London bears the inscription: "Muzio Clementi Called The Father Of The Pianoforte"...   Amongst his major works are over 60 piano sonatas, sonatinas and the study *Gradus ad Parnassum*. His sonatinas Op. 36, 37 and 38 remain in the standard piano teaching repertoire to this day. He also wrote 6 symphonies and a piano concerto. He was also a teacher, music publisher and piano manufacturer.

2nd Movement

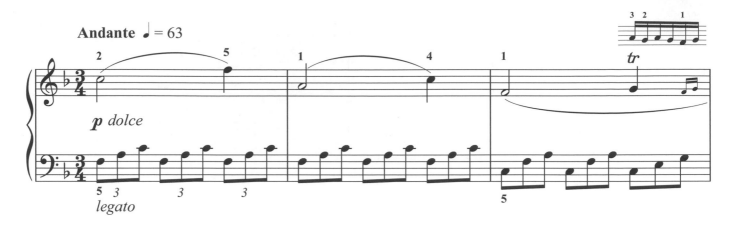

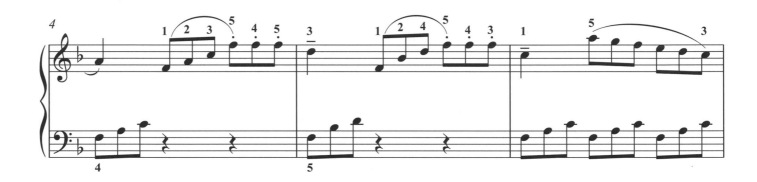

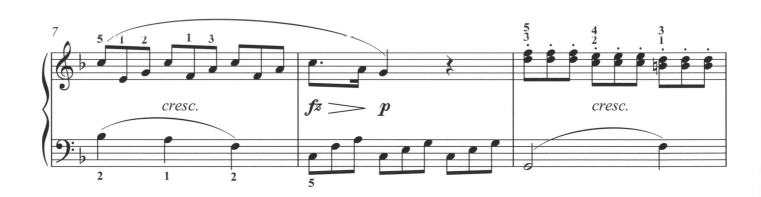

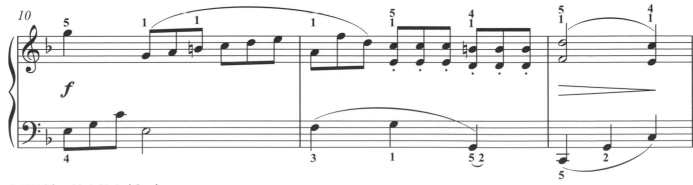

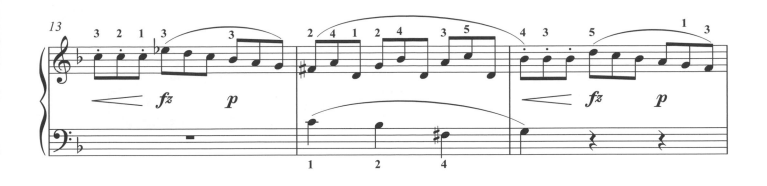

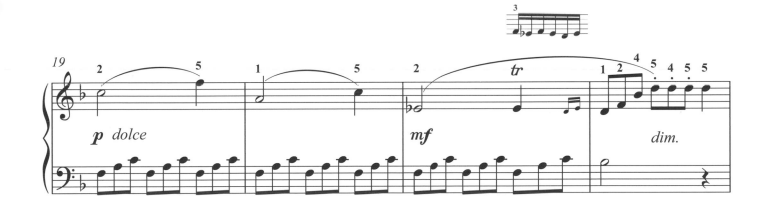

3rd Movement

Symphony

SYMPHONY

Surprise G Major Hob. I:94, theme fom the 2ⁿᵈ movement

Joseph Haydn (1732-1809)
Arr.: Hans-Günter Heumann

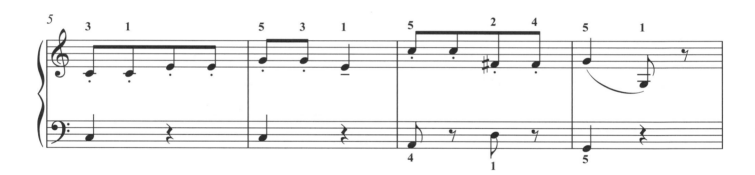

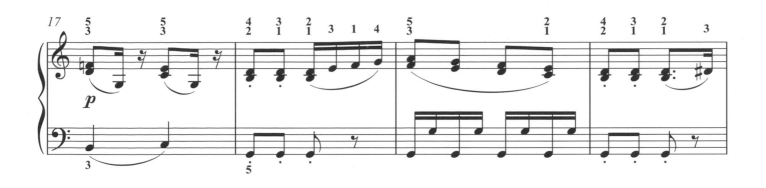

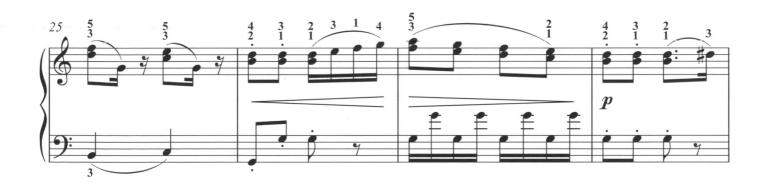

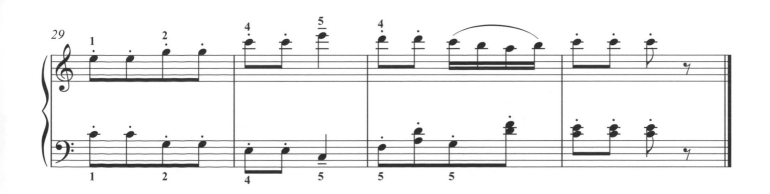

SYMPHONY

No. 9 D Minor Op. 125, *Ode to Joy*

Ludwig van Beethoven (1770-1827)
Arr.: Hans-Günter Heumann

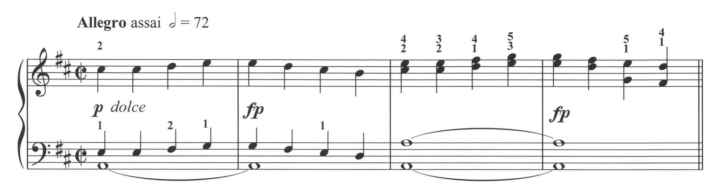

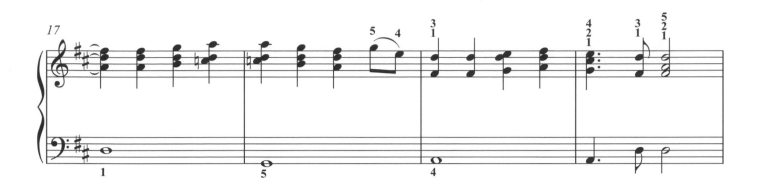

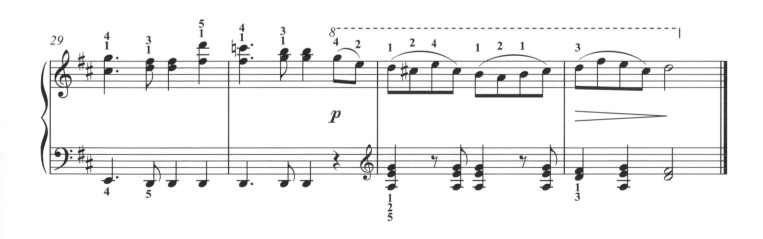

Solo Concerto

Concerto for Clarinet and Orchestra

A Major K 622, theme from the 2nd movement

Wolfgang Amadeus Mozart (1756-1791)
Arr.: Hans-Günter Heumann

■ Technique Tip:

To emphasize the expressive melody of this famous adagio by Mozart, it is extremely important to make a distinction in dynamics between the melody, which leads in the right hand, and the accompanying left hand part.

To achieve, or develop a feel for this, the following exercise brings two different dynamics (f and p) together, first alternating, then with hands exactly together.

When you have mastered the technique and have achieved a satisfying interpretation, you may then add the pedal, as indicated, so that transitions are as smooth as possible.

Mozart composed this last solo concerto in September/ October 1791 in Vienna for the clarinettist and friend Anton Stadler.

String Quartet

SERENADE

String Quartet F Major Hob III:17,
theme from the 2nd movement

Joseph Haydn (1732-1809)
Arr.: Hans-Günter Heumann

RC + DC + FF ▸ More pieces in **Repertoire Collection**, **Duet Collection** and **Finger Fitness**, see page 108

Theory Check 3

1. The chromatic scale consists only of _____.

2. The period from c. 1750-1820 is known as _____.

3. Name the type of musical texture whereby one part leads and the others accompany:

   _____

4. Give another name for the classical period: _____

5. Name four important Classical musical forms: _____, _____,

   _____, _____.

6. Which instruments form the string quartet? _____, _____, _____, _____ .

7. The first movement of a sonata is usually in _____ form, which consists of three
   sections:

   _____, _____, _____ .

8. Which of these were famous Classical composers? Haydn, Diabelli, Schumann, Schubert, Chopin,
   Clementi, Beethoven, Tchaikovsky, Salieri

   _____

9. Which keyboard instrument was most popular in the middle of the 18th century?

   _____

10. Whose gravestone has the following inscription? ... *Called The Father Of The Pianoforte*?

   _____

11. Which composer wrote the "Surprise" symphony? _____

12. Which of the following instruments were *not* played in the classical orchestra, as used by Haydn and
    Mozart around 1790: flutes, oboes, clarinets, bassoons, piccolos, contrabassoon, horns, trumpets,
    trombones, triangle, cymbal, bass drum.

   _____

13. The first theme in the exposition in a major sonata is in the _____ and the second theme in

   the _____

14. The exposition always ends with a _____.

15. In the recapitulation both themes are in the _____.

See page 99 for answers

Lesson 11

Classical Crash Course 3

Stylistic Period: Romantic

In music history, the **Romantic Period** is the time **from c. 1820-1900.** It was a time in which composers allowed themselves to be particularly influenced by their imagination, feelings, and fairy tales, and expressed this in their music.

Public concert life continued to develop, and anyone who could afford to pay for a ticket was able to attend concerts. Musical events took place in concert halls, opera houses or in churches. In addition, salons and cafes became established where you could listen to music. Music in the home ('Hausmusik') was very popular. The piano was very much the leading instrument of the 19th century.

Important Musical Forms of Romantic Period

Programme music
In the romantic period, *programme music* (music related to extra-musical ideas) developed into an independent genre. Programme music makes particular use of tone painting - the representation of a painting with music. It includes the imitation of natural phenomena such as, for example, bird song (Beethoven's 6th symphony), a sun rise, or a storm. Programme music tells a story, or describes particular events, such as in *Vltava* (*The Moldau*) by Smetana, in which the course of the river is described.

Large symphonies, large operas
The romantic period adopted all the classical musical categories, albeit in an extended form. As a result many large symphonies and operas were composed.

Salon music
So-called *salon music* was developed, which was to some extent light, entertainment music, designed to be played in salons and coffee houses, particularly in Paris and Vienna.

Character pieces
In romantic piano music, the *character piece* played an important role. This was a short composition, the character of which was often described by the title: For example 'Wild Horseman' (*Wilder Reiter*), 'Dreaming' (*Träumerei*), and the 'Pleading Child' (*Bittendes Kind*) by Schumann.
The character piece aims to capture a particular feeling or affect.

Art song
The German art song – *Kunstlied* – reached its culmination in the romantic period with the composers Schubert, Schumann, Brahms and Wolf. The singer is usually accompanied by the piano.

The Romantic Orchestra

The Romantic orchestra was considerably larger than the Classical orchestra. A huge body of sound was created: new instruments were added and the number of instruments, particularly strings and wind, was increased. Berlioz and Wagner had a great influence on the sound of the Romantic orchestra in the 19th century. The large symphony orchestra is used today primarily for concert works of the late 18th to the early 20th century.

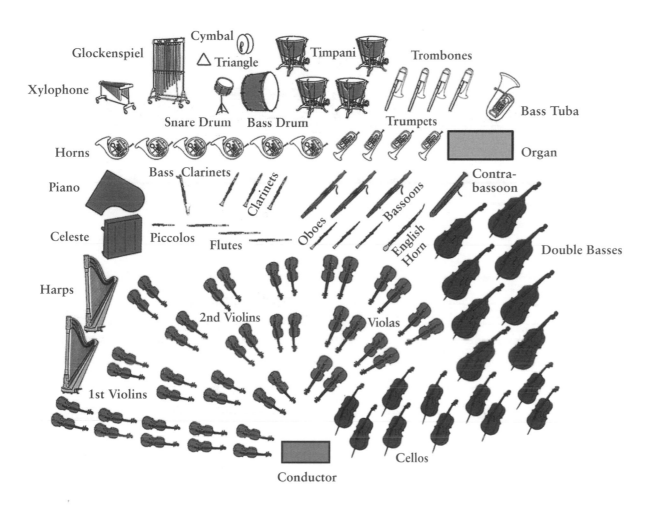

Famous Composers of the Romantic Period

Niccolò Paganini (1782-1840)

Carl Maria von Weber (1786-1826)

Franz Schubert (1797-1828)

Hector Berlioz (1803-1863)

Felix Mendelssohn Bartholdy (1809-1847)

Frédéric Chopin (1810-1849)

Robert Schumann (1810-1856)

Franz Liszt (1811-1886)

Richard Wagner (1813-1883)

Giuseppe Verdi (1813-1901)

Jacques Offenbach (1819-1880)

Bedřich Smetana (1824-1884)

Johann Strauss, Jr. (1825-1899)

Johannes Brahms (1833-1897)

Camille Saint-Saëns (1835-1921)

George Bizet (1838-1875)

Modest Mussorgsky (1839-1881)

Peter Ilyich Tchaikovsky (1840-1893)

Antonín Dvořák (1841-1904)

Edvard Grieg (1843-1907)

Giacomo Puccini (1858-1924)

Isaac Albéniz (1860-1909)

Gustav Mahler (1860-1911)

Programme Music

A Ball

Symphonie fantastique Op. 14,
theme from the 2nd movement

Hector Berlioz (1803-1869)
Arr.: Hans-Günter Heumann

Waltz
Allegro non troppo ♩. = 60

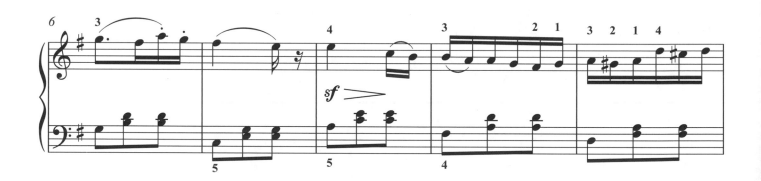

a tempo

Hector Berlioz
(1803-1869)

Country: France
Period: Romantic

Although Berlioz's musical talent was apparent from an early age, he first studied medicine and changed to study music at the *Paris Conservatoire* in 1826. In 1830 he won the highly acclaimed *Prix de Rome* at the Conservatoire. He proceeded to establish himself as a pioneer of romantic music with operas, choral works and symphonies. He deliberately exploited the tone colour of orchestral instruments with great knowledge and skill. His *Idée fixe* was a precursor of the *Leitmotiv*- a short, characteristic musical figure that, for example, frequently recurs in opera or in instrumental programme music, and has a particular significance, symbolizing a person, an object, an idea or feeling. He also wrote a comprehensive *Treatise on Instrumentation*. Berlioz was not only a composer and conductor, but also a music critic, however, he received little recognition during his lifetime. His most well-known works are: *Symphonie fantastique*, the dramatic legend *La damnation de Faust* and the Opera *Les Troyens*.

SYMPHONY "FROM THE NEW WORLD"

E Minor Op. 95, theme from the 2nd movement

Antonín Dvořák (1841-1904)
Arr.: Hans-Günter Heumann

Opera

NESSUN DORMA

Aria from the opera *Turandot*

CD 38

Giacomo Puccini (1858-1924)
Arr.: Hans-Günter Heumann

Giacomo Puccini
(1858-1924)

Country: Italy
Period: Romantic

At the age of 22, Puccini went to the Milan Conservatoire, graduating in 1883. He achieved worldwide success with his third opera *Manon Lescaut*, which brought him financial independence, enabling him to concentrate almost exclusively on composing operas. Of all Italian composers, Puccini's works are amongst those most often played. Typical characteristics of his operas are a dramatic plot, expressive and sensitive music, often foreign settings, colourful instrumentation and melodies of incomparable beauty.

His most famous operas are: *Manon Lescaut*, *La Bohème*, *Madame Butterfly*, and *Tosca* – one of the most famous works of the *Verismo* (Ital. *vero* = true, authentic) style. This is a style of opera that gained in popularity from 1890, and presented dramatic portrayals of contemporary social criticism and human passion. Sadly he was not able to complete *Turandot*.

Salon Music

THE MAIDEN'S PRAYER

Theme

Tekla Badarzewska-Baranowska (1834-1861)
Arr.: Hans-Günter Heumann

■ Playing Tips:

Play with each hand separately – first the right hand, then the left. Try to keep your wrist and hand relaxed while playing, in spite of the large stretches. Shake your hands between exercises to loosen up. In preparation for and whilst passing the thumb under and third finger over, move the wrist smoothly to the side.

FINGER FITNESS 9

CD 40

| **Tekla Badarzewska-Baranowska** (1834-1861)

Country: Poland
Period: Romantic | In her short life of only 27 years, Badarzewska-Baranowska achieved one of the great wonders in the history of piano music: with one single composition, *The Maiden's Prayer*, she gained great popularity in Europe, Asia and America, and so towards the end of the 19th century, this melody became perhaps one of the most successful piano pieces up until that time. Altogether Badarzewska wrote over 30 pieces for piano. |

Character Piece

WILD HORSEMAN

from *Album for the Young* Op. 68, No. 8

Robert Schumann (1810-1856)

FINGER FITNESS 10

Hans-Günter Heumann

Pastoral

Op. 100, No. 3

Friedrich Burgmüller (1806-1874)

The Acciaccatura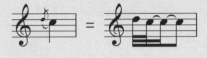

The acciaccatura is indicated by a small eighth note with a slash through the stem and flag, and from the mid-19th century was played before the beat. It is a short or fast ornament, taking little time away from the main note, which is emphasised. A variation of this ornament is the **double acciaccatura**, consisting of two notes before the main note.

Playing Tip:

This piano piece, with its wonderful singing pastoral melody has been deliberately conceived as a homophonic piece, to emphasize the melody over the chordal accompaniment. Play the melody very expressively and integrate the acciaccaturas smoothly and inconspicuously.

OLD FRENCH SONG

from *Children's Album* Op. 39, No. 16

Pjotr Ilyich Tchaikovsky (1840-1893)

Double Dotted Note

If a further dot is added to a dotted note, this adds half the value of the first dot. A double dotted quarter note therefore consists of a quarter note, an eighth note and a sixteenth note:

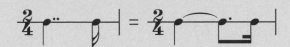

Art Song

HEIDENRÖSLEIN

Op. 3, No. 3, D 257

CD 45

Franz Schubert (1797-1828)
Poem by Johann Wolfgang von Goethe (1749 -1832)
Arr.: Hans-Günter Heumann

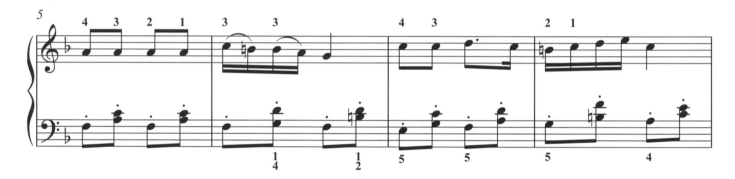

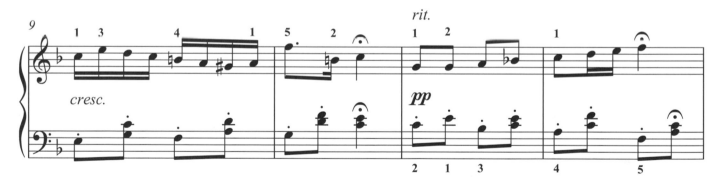

RC+DC+FF More pieces in **Repertoire Collection**, **Duet Collection** and **Finger Fitness**, see page 109

Theory Check 4

1. In music history, the Romantic period is from c. _____ .

2. Which instrument became particularly popular in the Romantic period, especially in the home?

   _____

3. Name four important musical forms in the Romantic period: _____ ,

   _____ , _____ , _____

4. What type of piece is, *Träumerei* by Schumann? _____

5. In which two cities was Salon music particularly popular during the Romantic period? _____ _____

6. Name two famous *Lied* (song) composers of the Romantic period: _____ , _____

7. Which musical form makes use of tone painting? _____

8. By whom is the work *Vltava* (*The Moldau*)? _____

9. Which two composers had significant influence on the sound of the Romantic orchestra?

   _____ , _____

10. Which of the following composers were *not* of the Romantic period: Wagner, Verdi, Brahms, Handel, Vivaldi, Grieg, Gluck, Mahler, Boccherini, Offenbach, Monteverdi, Schütz?

    _____

11. A precursor of the Leitmotiv was: _____

12. Who wrote the Opera *Tosca*? _____

13. A style of Italian opera at the end of the 19th century that gave dramatic portrayal of contemporary social criticism and human passion is called:

    _____

14. In her short life, the composer Badarzewska-Baranowska achieved a amazing feat: one of her compositions became famous around the world and was probably the most successful piano piece at the end of the 19th century. What is this work called?

    _____

15. A double dotted quarter note consists of: _____ , _____ , _____ .

See page 99 for answers

Lesson 12
Polyrhythms

Polyrhythms are the simultaneous occurrence of different rhythms. Certain forms are known as 'conflict' rhythms, for example duplets against triplets, a common feature of much piano music.

The rhythm and sound is identical:

If you combine the rhythms and present them on one level, you obtain the following rhythm:

Although the presentation of duplets against triplets – commonly known as two against three – looks very complicated in notation (examples 1 and 2), the structure can be simplified (examples 3 and 4).

Rule: The second duplet note comes in between the second and third triplet note.

Divided between the hands, it looks like this (always think of the rhythm and feel it as in examples 3 and 4):

FINGER FITNESS 11

Hans-Günter Heumann

PRELUDE

Op. 28, No. 4

Frédéric Chopin (1810-1849)

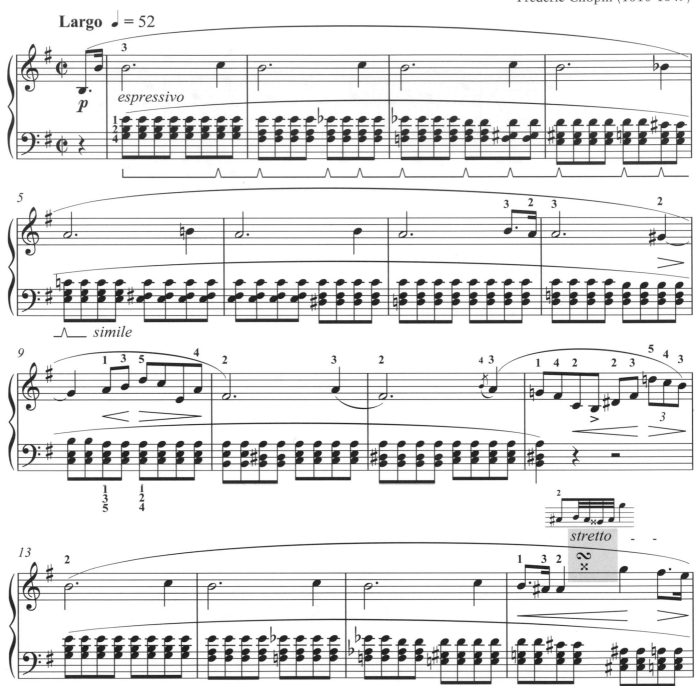

stretto = push on, speed up, hurry

smorz. = **smorzando** = restrained, dying away, gradually slowing down

Double sharp: ✗
A double sharp sign indicates that the note should be raised by two half tone (semitone) steps. For example, the note G becomes **G double sharp**.

The turn ∾
The **turn** is an ornament whereby the upper and lower neighbouring notes are played around the main note in a group of four. Take care with accidentals!

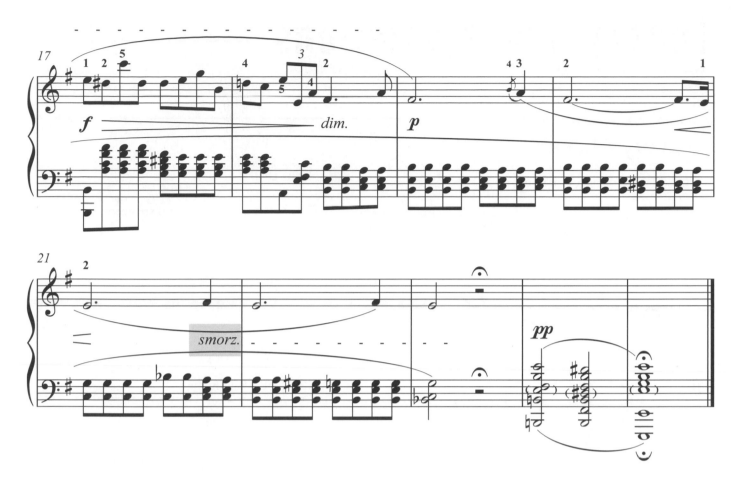

The **24 Preludes Op. 28** are a piano cycle composed by Chopin between 1836 and 1839. This work was related to *The Well-Tempered Clavier* by J. S. Bach in that it goes through all major and minor keys. The **fourth prelude** is one of his most well-known as well as one of his easiest pieces. It has a yearning melody and due to the descending chromaticism and the key of E minor, has a resigned, depressive, hopeless effect. Chopin wished to have this played at his funeral, along with Mozart's Requiem.

Frédéric Chopin
(1810-1849)

Country: Poland
Period: Romantic

By the age of seven, Chopin had already composed two polonaises. At the age of eight he often played in public and was hailed as a 'wunderkind'. Chopin's path to a career as a virtuoso began in Warsaw in 1827 and continued in Vienna in 1829. From 1831 Chopin lived and worked – as a famous pianist and teacher – in Paris, where he became an attraction of the high society. Here he became acquainted with other important musicians such as Liszt and Berlioz. Due to ill health he spent the winter months of 1838/39 on the island of Majorca accompanied by the writer George Sand, with whom he had a relationship. In 1848 Chopin travelled to give concerts in London and Scotland and returned completely exhausted to Paris, where he died one year later. Chopin created a new virtuoso piano style incorporating many ornaments, expressive melodies and a poetic sound. His compositions were primarily for the piano. Amongst his works are 2 piano concertos, 3 piano sonatas, preludes, waltzes, studies, nocturnes, mazurkas, polonaises, ballades and scherzos.

FF ▶ More pieces in **Finger Fitness**, see page 109

Theory Check Solutions

Theory Check 1

1. Low held or accompanying notes.

2.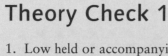

3.

4. 1

5.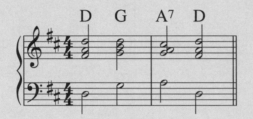

6. B♭ D♭ F

7. rallentando, ritardando, stringendo, accelerando

8.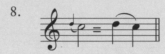

9. Portato

10. Robert Schumann

Theory Check 2

1. Polyphony, in which individual voices are melodically and rhythmically independent.

2. Basso continuo, concerto grosso, ornamentation, polyphony

3. Concertino

4. Bach, Vivaldi

5. The figured bass period

6. Fugue

7. Claudio Monteverdi

8.

9. A musical figure that is repeated, stepwise, at a higher or lower pitch

10. Note above

11. Mordent

12. No

13. The smaller the denominator, the slower the tempo.

14. It indicates the emotional condition

15. Clavichord, Cembalo, Spinet, Virginal, Organ

16. George Frideric Handel

17. Suite

18. Florentine Camerata

19. Recitative

20. Cantata

Theory Check 3

1. Half tones (semitones)

2. The Classical period

3. Homophony

4. Viennese Classical period

5. Sonata, symphony, solo concerto, string quartet

6. 2 violins, 1 viola, 1 violoncello

7. Sonata form: exposition, development, recapitulation

8. Haydn, Diabelli, Clementi, Beethoven, Salieri

9. Hammer Piano

10. Muzio Clementi

11. Joseph Haydn

12. Piccolos, contra bassoon, trombones, triangle, cymbals, bass drum

13. Tonic, dominant

14. Repeat sign

15. Tonic

Theory Check 4

1. c. 1820-1900

2. Piano

3. Programme music, salon music, character pieces, art song (Lied)

4. Character piece

5. Paris, Wien

6. Schubert, Schumann

7. Programme music

8. Bedřich Smetana

9. Berlioz, Wagner

10. Handel, Vivaldi, Gluck, Boccherini, Monteverdi, Schütz

11. Idée fixe

12. Giacomo Puccini

13. Verismo

14. The Maiden's Prayer

15. Quarter note (crotchet), eighth note (quaver), sixteenth note (semiquaver)

Piano Warm-ups
Scales, Chords and Arpeggios

These exercises improve your **technical skills** (evenness, accuracy, finger strength and independence, speed) and **theoretical knowledge** as well as your **listening skills**.

C Major

A Harmonic Minor

G Major

E Harmonic Minor

D Major

B Harmonic Minor

F Major

D Harmonic Minor

Bb Major

G Harmonic Minor

Chromatic Scale

Glossary

accelerando .... *accel.* .... Gradually getting faster (speed up)

Acciaccatura .... 𝄼 .... A small eighth note with a slash through the stem and flag, which from the mid-19th century was played before the beat, shortening the main beat accordingly. The main note should be emphasized.

Agogics .... Generic term for changes of tempo that bring a composition to life.

Appoggiatura .... A small note, written before the main note. It begins on the beat of the main note and shortens this accordingly. The duration of the appoggiatura is generally half the value of the main note, or two-thirds if it is a dotted note.

Arpeggio .... The notes of a chord are played one after another, like a harp (Ital. arpa = harp), rather than all together.

Baroque .... Period from c. 1600-1750

Bordun .... Low held or accompanying notes

Cantata .... A vocal work in several movements with instrumental accompaniment. The texts may be sacred or secular.

Character piece .... A short composition that aimed to capture a particular feeling or effect

Chromatic scale .... Scale consisting of half tones (semitones)

Chromaticism .... Series of semitone steps in a melody

Classical period .... Period from c. 1750-1820

Concertino .... Small group of instruments, usually consisting of three solo instruments.

Concerto grosso .... Main form of instrumental music in the baroque period. The large orchestra (tutti) and a small group of instruments – the so-called 'concertino' – play alternately.

Double sharp .... × .... A double sharp sign indicates that the note is to be raised by two semitone steps or half steps.

Figured bass
(basso continuo) .... Term for a continuous bass part accompanying a melody.

Florentine Camerata		A group of well-educated men who met in Florence, around 1600, with the aim of bringing Greek drama to life again.
Fughetta		Term for a little fugue
Fugue		A piece with several voices, which adheres to strict rules, and requires great skill to compose.
Homophony		A way of writing in which all voices are rhythmically synchronized or in which a melody is accompanied by chords.
Ländler		Ländler is the term for an Austro-Bavarian folk dance from around 1800 in a gentle 3/4-time. It consists of two repeated 8-bar sections.
Mordent		An ornament consisting of a simple change from the main note to its neighbour and back.
Oratorio		A composition in several sections for choir, soloists and orchestra, similar in form to opera, but, usually with biblical themes.
Polyphony		The term for pieces in many parts in which the Individual parts, or voices, are melodically and rhythmically independent.
Polyrhythms		The simultaneous occurrance of different rhythms.
portato		A form of articulation whereby the notes should be played neither legato nor staccato, but each note should be played with a little emphasis.
Programme music		Music related to extra-musical ideas.
rallentando	*rallent. / rall.*	Getting slower
ritenuto	*riten.*	Hold back, hesitate
Romantic period		Period from c. 1820-1900
Salon music		Often light entertainment music, played in salons and coffee houses.
Sarabande		A courtly festive, serious dance in 3/2 or 3/4 time with characteristic emphasis on the 2nd beat. It was a fixed part of the suite in baroque music.
smorzando	*smorz.*	Restrained, dying away, gradually slow down

Sonata		A sonata consists of three or four movements. The first movement is generally in so-called sonata form, which consists of an exposition, development and recapitulation.
Sonatina		The term for a short, relatively easy sonata.
stretto		Push on, speed up
String quartet		A musical ensemble consisting of: 2 violins, 1 viola, 1 violoncello
stringendo	*string.*	Gradually getting faster
Suite		A composition in many parts, consisting of a series of dances.
Tempo rubato		Although the note values are the same, they the notes should be played irregularly - a little hesitantly or slightly faster.
Terrace dynamics		Abrupt, stepwise dynamics
Thirty-second note / Demisemiquaver	♪	The thirty-second note has a filled note head with a stem and three flags.
Trill	⌇ ⌇ *tr*	Ornament produced by quickly alternating the main note and its upper neighbour note.
Turn	∾	Ornament whereby the upper and lower neighbouring notes are played around the main note in a group of 4.
Verismo		A style of opera that gained popularity in Italy from 1890, which gave dramatic portrayal of contemporary social criticism and human passion.

Further Repertoire RC+DC+FF

You can supplement the following lessons of **The Classical Piano Method: Book 3** with material from the accompanying volumes: **Repertoire Collection 3 (ED 13573)**, **Duet Collection 3 (ED 13583)** and **Finger Fitness 3 (ED 13553)**.

LESSON 2

Repertoire Collection 3: The Ballet (D. G. Türk)

German Dance Hob. IX:12, No. 8 (J. Haydn)

Duet Collection 3: Rondino Op. 149, No. 17 (A. Diabelli)

Ballad Op. 99, No. 3 (A. Gretchaninov)

Finger Fitness 3: School of Velocity Op. 141, No. 4 (C. Gurlitt)

LESSON 3

Finger Fitness 3: Finger Strength and Equalization of all Fingers: 1, Exercise No. 4 (C.-L. Hanon)

Finger Strength and Equalization of all Fingers: 2, Exercise No. 5 (C.-L. Hanon)

LESSON 4

Repertoire Collection 3: In the Hall of the Mountain King (E. Grieg)

The Cuckoo (F. Couperin)

Duet Collection 3: Russie (J.-B. Weckerlin)

Finger Fitness 3: Wrist Rotation Exercise (H.-G. Heumann)

Praeludium harpeggiato (J. K. F. Fischer)

LESSON 5

Repertoire Collection 3: The New Doll Op. 39, No. 9 (P. I. Tchaikovsky)

Duet Collection 3 Polonaise Op. 87, No. 50 (H. Wohlfahrt)

Finger Fitness 3: First Instructor Op. 599, No. 49 C. Czerny)

Easy Etude Op. 108, No. 25 (L. Schytte)

LESSON 6

Repertoire Collection 3: Polonaise (Anonymous, BWV Anh. 119)

Duet Collection 3: Minor and Major (D. G. Türk)

The Eel Snakes Through the Water (P. I. Tchaikovsky)

Finger Fitness 3: Passacaille Var. 8 + 9 HWV 432, No. 7 (G. F. Handel)

Left and Right Hand Melody (H.-G. Heumann)

Elegy Op. 201, No. 10 C. Gurlitt)

LESSON 7

Finger Fitness 3:   Elementary Study Op. 176, No. 20 (J.-B. Duvernoy)

LESSON 8

Repertoire Collection 3:   Lascia ch'io pianga (G. F. Handel)

See, the Conquering Hero Comes (G. F. Handel)

Sinfonia (J. S. Bach)

Fuga in C Major (J. Pachelbel)

Canon in D Major (J. Pachelbel)

Duet Collection 3:   La Caccia (A. Vivaldi)

Air (G. F. Handel)

Finger Fitness 3:   Solfeggio (J. C. F. Bach)

Easy Exercise Op. 139, No. 42 (C. Czerny)

First Instructor Op. 599, No. 65 (C. Czerny)

Preparatory School Op. 101, No. 101 (F. Beyer)

LESSON 9

Finger Fitness 3:   Allegretto Op. 823, No. 40 (C. Czerny)

The Whirlwind Op. 64, No. 9 (J. L. Streabbog)

LESSON 10

Repertoire Collection 3:   Sonatina in G Major Op. 36, No. 2 (M. Clementi)

Sonatina in G Major WoO Anh. 5, No. 1 (L. van Beethoven)

Symphony No. 7 (L. van Beethoven)

Concerto for Piano and Orchestra D Major (J. Haydn)

Musette (L. Mozart)

Minuet Hob. IX:8, No. 12 (J. Haydn)

Ecossaise in Eb Major WoO 86 (L. van Beethoven)

Duet Collection 3:   The Birdcatcher's Song (W. A. Mozart)

Duettino No. 9 (J. B. Vanhal)

Sonatina in D Major (D. G. Türk)

Turkish March (L. van Beethoven)

Finger Fitness 3:   Finger Strength and Equalization of all Fingers: 3, Exercise 6 (C.-L. Hanon)

Finger Strength and Equalization of all Fingers: 4, Exercise 7 (C.-L. Hanon)

Prelude and Exercise Op. 46, No. 1 (M. Clementi)

Bagatelle Op. 119, No. 9 (L. van Beethoven)

Three Little Studies Op. 821, No. 1-3 (C. Czerny)

LESSON 11

Repertoire Collection 3: Anxious Heart Op. 47, No. 5 (R. Fuchs)

Theme and Variations in A Major (T. Kullak)

Symphony No. 7 "Unfinished" (F. Schubert)

La donna è mobile (G. Verdi)

Soft lament Op. 100, No. 16 (F. Burgmüller)

Sicilian Op. 68, No. 11 (R. Schumann)

Waltz Op. 18, No. 6, D 145 (F. Schubert)

Prelude Op. 28, No. 6 (F. Chopin)

Duet Collection 3: Ländler D 366, No. 4 (F. Schubert)

Ländler D 366, No. 5 (F. Schubert)

Miniatur Op. 93, No. 3 (R. Fuchs)

Marcia Op. 3, No. 5 (C. M. von Weber)

Little Piece WAB 124, No. 2 (A. Bruckner)

Little Piece WAB 124, No. 3 (A. Bruckner)

Birthday March Op. 85, No. 1 (R. Schumann)

En plus (E. Satie)

Finger Fitness 3: Postludium Op. 210, No. 34 (C. Gurlitt)

Ballad Op. 100, No. 15 (F. Burgmüller)

Arietta Op. 201, No. 9 (C. Gurlitt)

First Instructor Op. 599, No. 71 (C. Czerny)

L'agilité Op. 20, No. 10 (F. Le Couppey)

The Wagtail Op. 100, No. 11 (F. Burgmüller)

Cross Hand Etude (H.-G. Heumann)

Distant Bells Op. 63, No. 6 (J. L. Streabbog)

Left Hand Studies Op. 89, No. 2 and 3 (H. Berens)

Etude Op. 24, No. 3 (F. Le Couppey)

Two Octave Arpeggios in the R. H. (H.-G. Heumann)

Two Octave Arpeggios in the L. H. (H.-G. Heumann)

Allegretto Op. 82, No. 67 (C. Gurlitt)

Moderato Op. 82, No. 66 (C. Gurlitt)

Little Study Op. 71, No. 6 (T. Kirchner)

Little Study Op. 71, No. 18 (T. Kirchner)

Étude Enfantine Op. 37, No. 14 (J.-H. Lemoine)

Children's Study Op. 79, No. 1 (H. Berens)

LESSON 12

Finger Fitness 3: Easy Exercise Op. 139, No. 74 (C. Czerny)

CD Track Listing

1	The Linden Tree / Pattern 1
2	The Linden Tree / Pattern 2
3	The Linden Tree / Pattern 3
4	The Linden Tree / Pattern 4
5	The Linden Tree / Pattern 5
6	Finger Fitness 1
7	Country Dance
8	Musette
9	Lullaby / Pattern 5
10	Finger Fitness 2
11	After the Ball
12	Finger Fitness 3
13	Allegro
14	Finger Fitness 4
15	The Sick Doll
16	Minuet
17	Ombra mai fù
18	Prepare Thyself, Zion
19	Finger Fitness 5
20	Finger Fitness 6
21	Zion Hears the Watchmen Calling
22	Prelude BWV 939
23	Pastorale
24	Finger Fitness 7
25	Sarabande
26	Fughetta
27	Finger Fitness 8
28	Entry of the Gladiators
29	Sonatina in C Major Op. 36, No. 1 / 1st movement
30	Sonatina in C Major Op. 36, No. 1 / 2nd movement
31	Sonatina in C Major Op. 36, No. 1 / 3rd movement
32	Symphony "Surprise"
33	Symphony No. 9, Ode to Joy
34	Concerto for Clarinet and Orchestra
35	Serenade
36	A Ball
37	Symphony "From the New World"
38	Nessun dorma
39	The Maiden's Prayer
40	Finger Fitness 9
41	Wild Horseman
42	Finger Fitness 10
43	Pastoral
44	Old French Song
45	Heidenröslein
46	Finger Fitness 11
47	Prelude Op. 28, No. 4

Recording Acknowledgments

Recorded January 2014
Piano – Samantha Ward
Engineered and Mixed by Dick Hammett,
Red Gables Studios

Keyboard Notation System

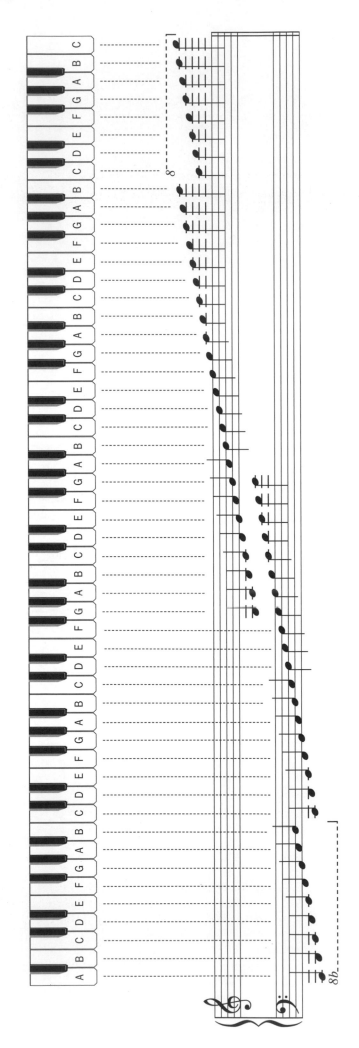